# THE NATIONAL POETRY SERIES

The National Poetry Series was established in 1978 to ensure the publication of five poetry books annually through participating publishers. Publication is funded by the Lannan Foundation; Stephen Graham; Joyce & Seward Johnson Foundation; Glenn Schaeffer; Juliet Lea Hillman Simonds Foundation; Tiny Tiger Foundation; and, Charles B. Wright III. This project also is supported in part by an award from the National Endowment for the Arts, which believes that a great nation deserves great art.

NATIONAL
ENDOWMENT
FOR THE ARTS

## 2006 COMPETITION WINNERS

Laynie Browne of Oakland, California, *The Scented Fox*
Chosen by Alice Notley, Wave Books

Noah Eli Gordon of Denver, Colorado, *Novel Pictorial Noise*
Chosen by John Ashbery, HarperCollins

Laurie Clements Lambeth of Houston, Texas, *Veil and Burn*
Chosen by Maxine Kumin, University of Illinois Press

Mart⌐ ⌐ ⌐ *Vertigo*
Ch ⌐ Press

William ⌐ *us Systems*
Chos ⌐ Books

# VERTIGO

### POEMS
## Martha Ronk

Coffee House Press
MINNEAPOLIS

Coffee House Press books are available to the trade through our primary distributor, Consortium Book Sales & Distribution, 1045 Westgate Drive, Saint Paul, MN 55114. For personal orders, catalogs, or other information, write to: Coffee House Press, 27 North Fourth Street, Suite 400, Minneapolis, MN 55401.

Coffee House Press is a nonprofit literary publishing house. Support from private foundations, corporate giving programs, government programs, and generous individuals helps make the publication of our books possible. We gratefully acknowledge their support in detail in the back of this book.

Good books are brewing at coffeehousepress.org

LIBRARY OF CONGRESS CATALOGING-IN-PUBLICATION DATA
Ronk, Martha
Ronk, Martha Clare.
Vertigo / Martha Ronk.
p. cm.
ISBN-13: 978-1-56689-205-6 (alk. paper)
ISBN-10: 1-56689-205-8 (alk. paper)
I. Title.
PS3568.O574V47 2007
811'.54—DC22
2007017784

FIRST EDITION | FIRST PRINTING
1 3 5 7 9 8 6 4 2
Printed in the United States

# VERTIGO

## PART I

"I cannot remember anything about this journey other than this"

## PART II

It is no more a world to us

PART III
"It was quite as if, she explained, the voices were unreal"

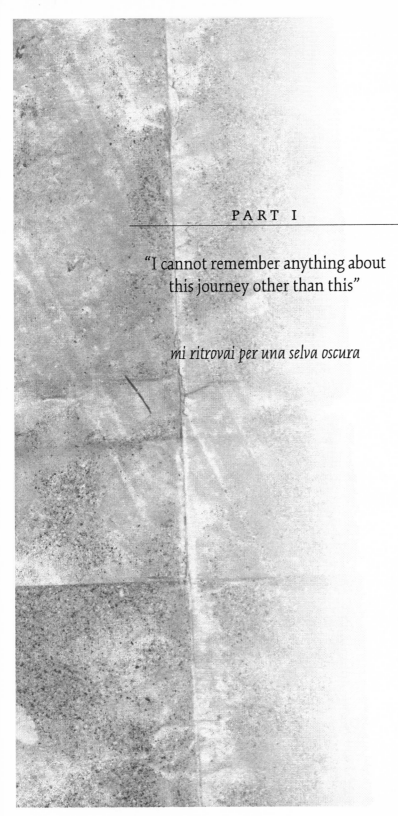

## PART I

"I cannot remember anything about
this journey other than this"

*mi ritrovai per una selva oscura*

**"I cannot remember anything about this journey
other than this"**

A moment of inattention brought it all back as in the dream
it catches in your throat and you jerk back from the edge or
hear the cry from someone else although the scene is eerily
quiet almost everywhere. The more images I gathered from the past
the more unlikely it seemed that the past had actually happened
in this way or that, but rather one had pulled back from the edge
and for that moment it all came rushing in.
Events that might have happened otherwise play themselves out
in ways that begin to seem familiar as if the sentence itself
by the one word turned the stream as a jutting rock might do.
I see a man fishing and I see the line spooled out
over his head in beautiful figure eights as if I were practicing
my hand in the school my mother went to before I was born.

**"So they say: 'This is what happened'; but they do not say what the person was like to whom it happened."**

She says she has had a bad day and I see myself
knocking about with windows letting in strange light.
If I pushed up against frames from that earlier time
the windows would explain themselves.
What she couldn't explain amounts to a theory of sorts,
the early crows piercing the fog like coughs,
the windows becoming vaguer by the moment.
One struggles toward glass,
the bits of unscraped paint,
leftover blues and grays thickening,
the wings of frantic birds.
One tries to get through, French doors somersaulted into,
the door as a way into it was about evening then.
There was a mirror as well but it only explains finger words
erased, breath fogging it over.

## "The grayness of the early hours lasted almost until noon"

The crows are always there if this is where one lives.
So much for the principal parts of the story.
But it was not until two weeks later
I wrote about the birds, getting no response,
whereas in fact all is determined
by the most complex of interdependencies.
I told her they always woke me up when I was there
and she noted them but said she always slept through.
Then she began to acquire a bit more definition
later in the day and after I moved where the crows
from the gray cloud had done everything together
in the most ominous way. The association of the two
seems to have to do with sleeplessness,
with how so much earlier keeps hanging on.

**"It is only a question of discovering how we can get ourselves attached to it again"**

*a drawing by Vija Celmins*

I practice interruption to get used to it, get up to get the cup
and then sit down, go out to look at the sign on the corner, sit
down, open the book to 37, *Moon Surface (Luna 9),* close
it, open my mouth to get used to what it says and then
in some weathers, it's offered up freely and you have to
cover the books in plastic, remember to take it with you just in case
and you have to be grateful not to think things up.
Her surface drawings put one squarely on the moon
and there's nothing to take your mind off it, no one brings coffee,
and she's reminded of a scene where the actor talks about how
he's scared to leap off a balcony and then he finally leaps.
Someone keeps coming to the door, someone makes a mark
like graphite until it builds up slowly on the surface.

## "I keep looking in the windows when I walk by"

When she crosses under the Gulf sign with her folded umbrella
    in the bright sun.
When she sees the limp hair of the swimmer.
When she holds her limp umbrella next to the limp dress.
Others have their morning routines, cayenne pepper in green tea,
a walk from hither to yon, repeated rituals of ruin
as if we mourn our own demise daily in the thick of it.
A book with photographs of crumbling columns,
stone facades broken into phantom bits,
an entire day given over to dust and shaking out the rain
from the spines of the umbrella, from the torn parka she put
    in the play.
I keep looking in the windows when I walk by hoping to see how
    to do it.
If I see the body I was looking for it is almost always mine.

## "This sense of numbness soon came over me"

*Out-of-touch* is the literal phrase one might use
even passing by the boxwood with hands outspread,
running along the vines, the tendrils hanging,
leaves sodden with rain.
There are never enough pages to describe
the expanse of a valley where a low-lying cloud
rims the view and blankets out everything one might see.
He seems ill as the trees, so close to the edge of a life
that his companion at dinner remembers his argument
that portraiture freezes the eyes until the passerby has to look back.

## "The sounds in and of themselves were less like the sounds of anyone"

Walking the stone path in the dark I had to keep
my eyes fixed for if I lifted them
to see where I was going all was a dense black
whereas if I looked down, the reflection off the gravel
made it possible to hear the sounds my feet made
as I made my way slowly toward a fixed point of light
I could not yet make out the night was so dense.
The sound of the bird seemed broken.
I little knew what to expect.
The time had been set, but given the unpredictable nature
of the principal parts of the story,
the sounds in and of themselves
were less like the sounds of anyone walking
than of noise at an open door,
the bird signaling what never would be.

**"I've often felt that I have no place in reality"**

*what bootes it that I was sith now I am but weedes and wastfull gras.*
—Edmund Spenser

Shades are everywhere wearing green shoes or the felt slippers
they favor and I can't even think to leave off the "the" despite being
in a kind of hurry to get where it is I want to get to,
sanding the places the rain came and peeled onto the floor,
the white one painted like the deck of a ship
someone might sail in one day that came sooner than I'd thought.
They stand at the rail with the moon wrapped around them
and nothing seems as close at hand as the shades of those long gone
and pursing their lips at the very moment I've turned them on
running through meadows, the *weedes and wastfull gras.*

## "I managed nonetheless to find my way rather blindly"

More and more I felt impelled to look over at her
and as she read more and more I felt it was time to leave
but was unable to imagine actually getting up from my table
and crossing the room. It's often so like a stage the simple room
one must cross to the door to the hall to the door
leading to the outside. It seemed to me then that one
could simply end one's life by retreating into one's mind
and stunned as I was by the sunlight upon leaving the building
I managed nonetheless to find my way rather blindly to the quiet
of my own apartments where I found she hadn't
managed to leave and had left as I time and again
have reminded her not to, all the stage lights burning.

**"Self-regard played across the walls of the room like shadows "**


We become unpleasant to ourselves the moment we gain
      some distance
from what we were and it happens regularly these days
as if a microscope were shifting objects in size,
as if it were a hot night and the moth fallen into the crevice of a book
were moving across the sentence as the letters melt
under the influence of bark-like wings,
the alternating batter of light and shade.
To the left side of the small room, a shadow rises
from the halo of the lamp and shifts with the slight wind
as the edge of the flyleaf disappears on the other side.
One remembers things long forgotten and the world is flat.

## "We hit an impasse on the trail going up"

*ou sont les neiges d'antan*


The collapse of the trees in the snow—
when was the last time I didn't just read about snow.
We hit an impasse on the trail going up early May
the usual effort to ward off the fear of precipice made me tired
of the boys in their T-shirts.
The spooling of paper, the white of the snow,
the haircut that makes you think something's left out,
but he's just fixing it.
Impassive as statues we practice
reasonableness before it takes over again.
It's later now. It's harder to gather things up.
You remember them sitting by the sea watching it
and it seems almost reasonable.
You know something else is left out,
not just the years of falling snow.

## "It seemed similar to choice, although in an adjacent register"

Ferns and jewelweed fanning the air too slowly for the coming shift
as if the package as yet unwrapped had already arrived
in another time zone, the desert hot and dry.
Anticipation veiled what could be seen from the window.
We remained seated for about a quarter of an hour
counting the number of trees in order to put off the inevitable,
in order to see the effect the change would have before it happened
giving up what perhaps needn't have been given up,
selecting pain as one of the necessary elements,
not to lessen its effect, but to notice the precise moment of selection.

**"The headache alone forced me sometimes to the limit of consciousness"**

He says you had a bad night and it's as true as if I had told him
but by the time we speak the night has so receded
all oceans must have drained away.
Coleridge infuses voices in the night in ways
as understandable and flushed as writing plays.
Then the lingering sense of dread.
One of the characters must be prevented from collapsing into
the other and must be prevented from collapsing
entirely into the madness he finds so awfully attractive.
In the third act the noise level is such that it could have
     been morning
and they chime in at the top of their voices in midsentence
while afterwards and by the time we speak it's as silent as the sea.

**"Often, probably because I was so tired, the rain seemed
more than rain"**


Then all the pools were like nickels
until dark when the ashes
collapsed. Each time I lit up my face.
The downpour from the Keys and ruined trailers,
a roof flying across the headlines. Listen
to the unaware: water and wood.
She's waiting for it to leave.
He calls it by its common name, devil-in-the-mist.
It would startle itself if it could
with its repeated blues, its wired-on extensions,
hallucinations in the rain.
In the night the copper flashing holds,
the tea makes my mouth open and close
mechanical as any memory.

## "One wrong move is all it takes"

When I told my story all over again, it no longer sounded
plausible, even to me. Perhaps she did know what
she was talking about, perhaps I had been to St. Louis and seen
the painting of the androgynous Christ, and the painful
underpinnings of her life were perhaps clear to me although what
seemed more the case was that I had no way of
understanding the full import of the directions clearly written out
in pencil on lined yellow paper,
and yet in going over them again in my head the turmoil of
the night came back, the detail of the Victorian carpet,
palms fronds twisted on a maroon field,
and back stairs twisting up to where I had never been.

## "Twisting and turning like the ebbing tides"

*Amo, amas,* and the crossword puzzle takes off
even though the shift was not so entirely unexpected.
He looks troubled but it may be that she's the one
turning into the people sitting at the edge of the sea.
It's perhaps her mother checking the tide charts in the morning
and it's troubling even though one understands perfectly well
the need both for categories and the breaking of categories
one might like to have some latitude,
but the crossword puzzle is always there moving left and right
or up and down and the tide is coming in or going out
and to some extent we know it's hard-wired
and not just what happens to the body,
but the mind splashed by Latin and the Sargasso Sea.

**"The shadows of clouds scudded across the steep slopes and through the ravines"**

An almost theatrical obscurity seems to have settled on
the adjacent area usually described as ordinary and plain.
The field of weeds is overtaken by the constriction of one's chest,
concealed by rhapsodies. In these cases,
despite the numbers of internal distractions,
it is usually best to move about and although everywhere
there are great effusions of feeling, it is nonetheless
recommended to follow the last of the sunlight into that very field
even if the darkness itself is overtaking.
After a passage of time a light breaks on the scene
and allows one to exit in favor of the highly unusual
      display of clouds.

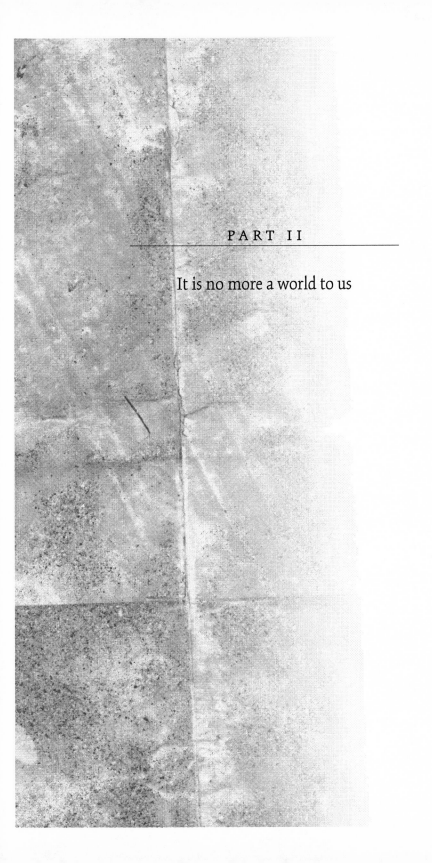

## PART II

It is no more a world to us

*With interstitial vacuities, a network of light.*


From the moment it was first seen as a bird
it was destined to always be a bird

and that is the way with constellations

and although the night sky is shapeless

we can make out a few stars although we
don't look up the words anymore.

*Cygnus* or *Swan* or *Roc* was his favorite
out by the sea you could see more clearly then.

One ought to be wary of one's examples or fathers for that matter

wearing the coat he was always wearing in the cold fog.

**The otherworldly**


                            The lecturer says
the Italians had it in their vowels, their food,

the fact, perhaps,

although he didn't say it, of cities lying on top of cities
excavating themselves from time to time to the inner regions of stone.

### It is no more a world to us

It's no more a world to us,
nor we any more people in it

when the building speaks,

the doors closing, the consonants collapsed,
the sounds of the sea in the city where a faucet fills an
      indentation in stone.

## The infinite number of conditions

In the portrait of Mme Cezanne, the border

of the wallpaper on the one side won't form

a straight line with that on the other.

Her hands are never still.

Outside it is spring with birds

almost everywhere you can't see but he claimed

you could see the softness, the hardness of objects,

even the smell of them

and the infinite number of conditions

each brushstroke must satisfy.

If she opens her mouth to speak in French,

if they are falling out of the sky,

if one is looking to the past for the meaning of the future

and to the future for how the line goes straight through her

and comes out the other side.

## Chants

Birds chant undeceiving things so it's impossible to attend

to anything on the far side of the wall where the maple puts
       forth leaves.

We had thought it over but today autumn red after rain.

All the ways I've used before useless or I'm stopped short in the place

before dark encountering such ordinary things.

It was that way in the park with all the birds when she said

of herself she never knew who it was who was speaking.

**Sky's**


Sky's an interruption

        thinking it through.

Looking up's a red sweater too small for the girl and the cloud hangs

        between one thought and another.

There's light through the window blocking out words coming closer

        and pronouncing the "t" at the end of the word.

Practicing a turn on the ice for hours, a cutout

        recovered in feet and ice.

**Any memory of**


Ferdinand of Medici married a princess you haven't any memory of

even the songs I'm told are the last to go after you've lost all else

although you suspect it has to be cemented in or built columnar

so that all the emotion in the world can't mar the fluting.

## A domestic geography


At the edge of the chair he tunes in channels of noise.

One might argue a visionary explanation

       as if the believers were right.

One is looking at a dish of pink roses

       latter-day saints on the road to perdition.

One is hiding in the closet trying to get away.

The noises are the ordinary ones of daily frets and reckonings

the toysound grackle of whatever bird.

She doesn't listen. He watches rapt.

Others go about their business as if they were mothers or fathers.

The knocking is from the believers

       or the bird you can't see tapping its way on the other side.

**If the glazes were iridescent**

We could have collected a number of things prior to that and then
      we could have arranged them

side by side if the glazes were iridescent and came from Ferrara
      where the girl rolls her hoop

down the endless street into open spaces where she got on the
      bus this morning

and went wherever they go when you can't see them anymore.

**In the Upper Reaches**

*"And so we try to subdue the disquieting existence of others"*
—Stendahl


Despite their fictional quality the characters are seemingly
in the process of making decisions
and moving themselves if not the clouds along
in the upper reaches where Stendhal praises those
beyond the idea of *perhaps.*

### They keep staring at the sky

*"Their eyes . . . remain raised to the sky"*
—"The Blind" Baudelaire


They keep staring at the sky as if,

having never seen it, they were

seeing it for the first time.

Without holding on the moon swings out

as the pointed feet of the people below

sweep their canes from side to side.

But the moon has unlimited bravado

and never flinches

as they make their slow way

over the pavement and up the curbs.

### Remoter Worlds

*"the everlasting universe of things / Flows through the mind"*
—Shelley


Some say remoter worlds visit us in sleep.

Thriving is the business of the mind.

*No shade of thee* in the willow the storm blew down.

Perhaps it's time to give over time to memorize.

How fine to think of each bird secure and in its place,

the mechanical wings of the owl,

swallows over the wire.

**In the space of**


Now the afternoon green of the sky before rain is here,
and even off the page it is about to rain
though the middle of the invisible sea
is not entirely clear
as one might say the sky is not,
yet what is that blue-gray reflection off
the water pitcher but wet as Florida always seems to be.

**The door opens**


One painter put a thick white line
where the door opens into the dark room
and women make beads and light stripes the floor.
Each time paint becomes light, we are asked to believe.
The requests come thicker of late.
They say one painter asked them to stand there,
hands out, the light coming in, for a long time
that is never long enough.

*Below the moon, above the sun*

from Sir Thomas Browne, *Selected Writings*


The greater part must be content

to be as though they had not been


Every houre addes


unto


which scarce stands one


moment.


*


like snow upon us


Wherein there is


nothing / *neige*

Many have taken voluminous pains to determine
the state of the soul


upon disunion


we find that


(and interred the ashes in a silver urne)


water was the originall of all things


\*


In vain                    , or


below the Moon


above the Sun


con-


trived          is lost in

a folly of                 memory


There is no antidote against the *Opium* of time, which temporally
considereth all things;



\*



But the most tedious being is that which can unwish itself,

content to be nothing, or never to have been

To subsist                , to live

to exist

                , and made one part of

                extasie      ever,

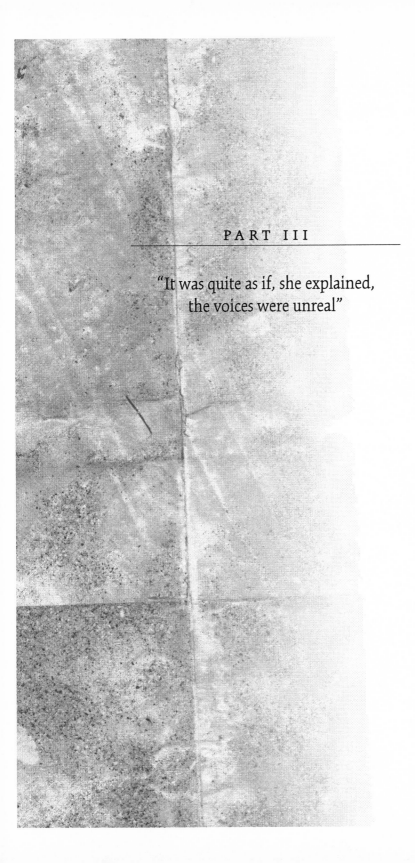

## PART III

"It was quite as if, she explained,
the voices were unreal"

**"I sat at the window and watched it cover everything by nightfall"**


The singer's voice's transparent as his skin.
The opium poppies fail;
one ashy petal falls.
We no longer choose pain,
not in the time that's left us, not like before.
When I close my eyes I see his chest lifting under the light shirt
breathing the Bach the organ breathes,
inhaling the porch, the after dinner, the taller trees
didn't used to be there in the earlier photographs.
The fugue is too large in the ashen hands of the tenor we
        can't talk about.
I am tired of getting over things.
The lightly brushed moth's a smudge on the bedsheet.
In the complete darkness it takes over the darkness—
his voice a color you could see through.

**"It was quite as if, she explained, the voices were unreal"**

Voices, she told me, like pine knots closely choked,
the slightly higher male voice she was certain took up
every limb. There it lay, to the right.
We remained for at least an hour watching the cloth
on the table fall out of the frame, the dancer's legs forming
beyond where anyone had thought to paint them.
Although she never spoke of this it was certain to me that she was
thinking as I was thinking and if the light had begun to flicker,
the other voices speaking just out of range would have
begun a cacophony of sound as unreal as the figure itself.

**"So on the landing to the first floor, I was, as it were, on the
borderline of what was permissible"**

Passing by is the startle of the world as the occasional
swallow or odor of musk. I don't remember where
the quotation is from or whose voice took me there
but when he moves across the floor it's the flight
off the wire and the haunting eyes of the portrait on the left wall
of the museum at Antwerp.
No matter how late the hour or the urgency of the request,
the composer hated being interrupted.
We could eat sweet salads and begin a kind of dissolution
we wouldn't want to see in others even if we could.
It could take shape as a figure speaking to one
who later explained the symphony downstairs to
someone wearing greenish rings and passing by.

## "You know how I am, he said, when it is getting late"

Mid-August lengthens.
Beethoven reaches the boy I'll never reach,
the clear O of the vowel, her extraordinary voice
as a fern at the edge of the road trilling in the wind.
He sits somewhere out of reach in the experience
he says don't you remember.
If we were all punctual we'd never arrive where we meant to go.
Once in a while we show up as if by chance along country roads
by mailboxes marked with handwritten signs,
and the bad translations of German songs.
On stage the woman is heavily poised in a silver dress.
Her singing calls up a similarly eerie and waterlogged sound.

## "I was astonished at the mysterious slow motion quality of the sound"

The water was at a standstill because of the severity of the wind,
taking on the glassy sheen described by authors who are moved by
    personal destiny
and buy photographic postcards to capture the touched-up beauty
in which moss is growing up the north side of the rock walls
extending like the Handel aria she sang, her voice a waterfall
reaching from the top beyond the line of vision into the chasm
    I fell into
in my dreams later that afternoon as I seem to keep falling into
no matter the various devices staged to prevent such an inexplicable
    loss of
balance and the sounds are stilled and by coincidence I feel it all
at this time of year as the shadows lengthen across the lawn.

## "Whenever she speaks to him in that voice, an infrequent enough occurrence"


What's the difference between trying to lift an arm and lifting
    an arm,
between desire and that other thing.  I'm glad to hear you're coming.
I am glad to hear you think you're coming despite the fact
she does take up the entire conversation, expressive as her dress
coming off in colors near the edge of every year she's ever been in.
Yet she talks during the entire playing of the cello piece
displacing it into what she wants us to hear and into the silence
written on her when she takes on your voice at dinner
when you'll arrive and now she speaks out of her beautifully
    disjointed face,
out of her hair wet from the pond, never in the voice she came
    in with.
When he lost his hearing, he heard only the cello's low notes
and what he heard changed his way of hearing the piece forever.

**"Cameras, he explained, came then to replace descriptive paragraphs"**

If description could outpace effusions of feeling,
serif or sans serif, punctuated with dashes and in Amherst,
could one say it was a peculiar summer.
I tried to like what I'd always liked and tried to get there
sooner rather than later.
I'd forgotten I liked orange until
on a scale of one to ten the petals ranged themselves
like swallows on the telephone wire
flying off at the sound of someone's coming.
Something should have been a topic—
I had thought it out and left nothing to chance,
but the people kept arriving
never thinking to find the appropriate word for
what they were taking in and writing down.
One snapped a lily between finger and thumb
and one had hair like spilling rust.

## "Also the photographs were out of focus, perhaps one had to conclude"

I was able to decipher only part of what she had written
in part because of the actual breaks in the paper, but in part
because of her use of foreign phrases interspersed in the text
to convey more precisely what it was she wanted to convey.
Also the photographs she had included as illustrations
were out of focus, perhaps one had to conclude, purposefully
but nonetheless, although clearly labeled as if from sixteenth-
century emblem books with names such as *Fortune* or *Faith*,
and quite impossible to match with the black-and-white
sailing ships, their masts ghostly and reaching beyond
the picture frame. She expected from me an immediate response
and I have waited *lo these many years* to give it.

## "The dead speak in pictures, some 19th-century figure keeps saying"

In the directions what's a pond, what a small body of water,
what happens when the paved road you're told to follow is gravel
and the sign is handscrawled and small where you were to go left.
The dead speak in pictures, some 19th-century figure keeps saying,
and there she is posing for a photograph
her high laced boot stuck out of the doorway as a lure.
The problem is a bewildering excess of trails:
left across the brook, up to the third marker at the gate
and still her face won't come clear.
By day they seemed quite ordinary pebbles around the pond
where the island floats, and illegibility is up for grabs.

**"It was a photograph of a house quite unlike any other I had inhabited"**


Loneliness is structural, at the base of the throat,
in the ribs that are suddenly gone, in the ache that reminds you
you are there when you hadn't been thinking about it
until the chair leg stands in the way you were going,
and spaces open gaudily up.
There is the coarse and grainy quality to something you'd rather
      not name—
the horizons extending and the brittle crack of joists
now small enough for the fire and the hearth of river rocks
      as slippery
as ashes in a house unimagined at the time as the past.

**"One night near Versailles, he turned as he took his leave"**
  (Atget)

It's the dark smudge where light doesn't strike the negative,
or erases the few leaves hanging in the bright alleyway.
Reflection might be an activity, might be the hour before sleep.
No one's narrating, but the talk at table goes on even after he's left.
You know how I am given a certain passage of time,
he said, I simply must, he said again, disappear.
In the center of the photograph, in the center of the pond
a horse lifts hoofs in the air: the startling freeze-frame of its
        marble mouth.

**"The photograph that reminds you how it is to be near the sea"**
  (Kertész)


If she is beautiful and never visits how is she like the one
who is not beautiful and never visits but in the dead
of winter when there is nowhere to go.
If she is beautiful as you describe
a woman I've never seen I want to own *Martinique 1972*
and the grainy view of what might be the sea.
But there we are the two of us sitting on the deck
overlooking something or other behind glass
when it arrives as always before you are ready
in a string of words that settles nothing
and not at all like the woman I had thought her to be.

**"Improbable as it may have seemed at the time"**
        (Stieglitz)


A black-and-white photograph is described as concave as if you could
        fall into it
or touch the shapes of objects not otherwise recognizable
as moving through painted rooms with one eye closed you will see
        seamless yellow all over
the blindness essential for any self-reflexive thought itself absent
        from the future
we talk about and write down on envelopes to keep it from
        collapsing in on itself
or taking off in that unpredictable direction along which fields
are arranged neatly enough and the clouds have equivalent
        consequences.

## "It seemed to all of us as remarkably like suspension in time"

Although the photo is from a town in Germany somewhere
I've never been to and the crowd full of unrecognizable
woolen coats and heavy shoes I'm reminded of those who stare
out at the uncomprehending array, the endless movements
and steamy air, as if I myself had stood at that station
with those valises, someone close-at-hand saying
*anonymity* or *anomie,* as if what drives them is a compulsion
to grasp the fleeting birds not in flight but in transition
from earth to air. They hover and flap, their suspension palpable.

**"All that remains in the left half of the painting is"**

The precision of color and even of symbols
announces a stance against which one can move either
closer or by indirection further away. If closer
then the meaning is clear and often labeled either
by custom or common knowledge, if farther
then the garments, painted in dark colors, merge
beyond recognition with the background, which is
equally unrecognizable. One doesn't know where one is
and cannot recall the name of one's maternal grandfather
or the person one knows as plainly as one's own hands
that themselves alternate between the indistinct
and the highly etched Dürer portraits of his own.

**Notes**

This book is in memory of Mary and Jack Ronk.

I would like to thank the MacDowell Colony where early versions of some poems were written.

Some of the titles are revised forms of sentences from W.G. Sebald's novels.

"I cannot remember anything about this journey other than this" for Paul Vangelisti.

"So they say: 'This is what happened'; but they do not say what the person was like to whom it happened" is for my sisters, Nancy Ihara and Patricia Flumenbaum (the title taken from "Sketches of the Past," by Virginia Woolf).

"We hit an impasse on the trail going up" is for Dale Wright.

"Any memory of" is for Susan Dworkin.

"The dead speak in pictures, some 19th-century figure keeps saying" for Jacob Lifson and Paulina Gatarz.

"I was astonished at the mysterious slow motion quality of the sound" for Joe Eck and Wayne Winterrowd.

"I've often felt that I have no place in reality" is for Tom Wudl.

# Acknowledgments

*ELN2 (Vol. 44.2 Fall/Winter 2006):* "The dead speak in pictures, some 19th century figure keeps saying," "It was a photograph of a house quite unlike any other I had inhabited," "The photograph that reminds you how it is to be near the sea," "Improbably as it may have seemed at the time," "It seemed to all of us as remarkably like suspension in time," "Also the photographs were out of focus, perhaps one had to conclude."

*Hambone* (forthcoming): "The photograph that reminds you how it is to be near the sea," "Suspension in time."

*The Laurel Review (Vol.40.2 Summer 2006):* "You know how I am, he said, when it is getting late."

*Boston Review (Vol.31.6 December 2006):* "I was astonished at the mysterious slow motion quality of the sound"

*Soft Targets (Vol. 1.1 2006):* "This sense of numbness soon came over me," "Self regard played across the walls of the room like shadows."

*14 Hills (Vol. 12 No. 1 Winter/Spring 2006):* "Sky's."

*Fascicle (on-line 2005):* "One night near Versailles he turned as he took his leave," "Often because I was so tired, the rain seemed more than rain," "The dead speak in pictures, some 19th-century figure keeps saying," "It seemed similar to choice, although in an adjacent register."

*A Rest chapbook, April 16 2005* for the reading at The Bowery 2005, selections.

*Ploughshares (Winter 2005):* "Cameras, he explained, came then to replace descriptive paragraphs."

*Volt (#11 2005)*: "The grayness of the early hours lasted almost until noon," "Whenever she speaks to him in that voice, an infrequent enough occurrence."

*APR (November/December 2004)*: "So they say: 'This is what happened'; but they do not say what the person was like to whom it happened," "It is only a question of discovering how we can get ourselves again attached to it," "We hit an impasse on the trail going up," "I sat at the window and watched it cover everything by nightfall," "I keep looking in the windows when I walk by."

*Interim (#22 2004)*: "The headache alone forced me sometimes to the limit of consciousness," "All that remains in the left half of the painting is," "The sounds in and of themselves were less like the sounds of anyone," "So on the landing to the first floor, I was, as it were, on the borderline of what was permissible."

*Prepositional, Seeing Eye Books (2004)*: "Remoter worlds," "For Odes (Shelley)."

*Radical Society (Vol. 20 #2 July 2003)*: "I cannot remember anything about this journey other than," "I managed nonetheless to find my way rather blindly," "The shadows of the clouds scudded across the steep slopes and through the ravines," "One wrong move is all it takes," "Also the photographs were out of focus, perhaps one had to conclude."

## Colophon

*Vertigo* was designed at Coffee House Press,
in the historic warehouse district of downtown Minneapolis.
The type is set in Kinesis.

## Funders

Coffee House Press is an independent nonprofit literary publisher. Our books are made possible through the generous support of grants and gifts from many foundations, corporate giving programs, individuals, and through state and federal support. This book was made possible in part, with a special project support from the National Poetry Foundation. Coffee House Press receives general operating support from the Minnesota State Arts Board, through an appropriation by the Minnesota State Legislature and from the National Endowment for the Arts, and major general operating support from the McKnight Foundation, and from the Target Foundation. Coffee House also receives support from: an anonymous donor; the Elmer and Eleanor Andersen Foundation; the Buuck Family Foundation; the Patrick and Aimee Butler Family Foundation; Stephen and Isabel Keating; the Lenfesty Family Foundation; Rebecca Rand; the law firm of Schwegman, Lundberg, Woessner & Kluth, P.A.; the James R. Thorpe Foundation; the Woessner Freeman Family Foundation; Wood-Rill Foundation; and many other generous individual donors.

*This activity is made possible in part by a grant from the Minnesota State Arts Board, through an appropriation by the Minnesota State Legislature and a grant from the National Endowment for the Arts.*

MINNESOTA
STATE ARTS BOARD

TARGET.

To you and our many readers across the country,
we send our thanks for your continuing support.

Good books are brewing at coffeehousepress.org